Salute the SON Little One

By Ashley W. Cummings

Illustrated by Gloria Jean Martin

Copyright 2021 Ashley W. Cummings

All Rights Reserved

This book is dedicated to Anaëlle B,
My beloved daughter,
born out of connecting with God
in the midst of struggle.
She is my vessel of hope and joy.

*I believe through conscious movement coupled with sincere, connected prayer,
one becomes still enough to hear the small voice of God.
This is where miracles are born.
May every reader of this book know the joy and peace found in movement, meditation, and prayer.*

Ashley W. Cummings

About the Author

Ashley Cummings is a wife, mom, social worker, trauma therapist, mental health consultant, and yoga teacher living in the suburbs of Houston, TX. She strives daily to stay connected to Sovereignty. Her prayer is for others to know the good love of God through both small and major miracles. Learn more at *dawncounsels.com*

About the Illustrator

GloriaJean was born and raised in Harrisburg, PA, where she began her creative explorations. She later ventured to Philadelphia to obtain her degrees in Illustration and Education. GloriaJean enjoys her passion in both art and education.

I breathe in deeply.
Arms upraised.
Tilt my head and
Give God praise.

I breathe out and forward fold.
I am forgiven,
I forgive.
I release every load.

I plant my hands
onto the ground,
Creating connection
to God's earth,

Then I slowly lower down.

Flat on the ground,
I rest and breathe.
I leave my cares to God.
I feel relieved.

Now I lift my head and heart,
Listening for wisdom
That God imparts.

I exhale and tuck my toes.
I lift my tailbone to the sky.
I take deep breaths in and out
- 1, 2, 3, 4, 5.
I remember I am strong,
And will do my best all day long.

I step my right foot forward,
Strong and steady.
The world is big,
But I am ready.

With my left foot forward,
I stand tall.
I am strong and stable.
I will not fall.

To bring balance before I end,
I begin and do this all again.
~ Repeat sequence ~

Criss cross legs
And hands to heart in prayer,
I'm reminded God loves me,
And always cares.

I remember to breathe
Throughout my day,
To create a calm and peace
filled pace.
Breathing is my saving grace.

Now I rise to stand,
Confident that
God always holds my hands.

Strong as a mountain,
Wise and free,
Now I am ready
For what the day brings me.

Pose 1 - Urdhva Hastasana Principle: Praise Scripture: Psalm 9:1

Pose 2 – Uttanasana Principle: Forgiveness, release Scripture: Matthew 6:12

Pose 3 - Plankasana
Principle: Surrender Scripture:
Romans 12: 1; James 4:7, 10

Pose 4 – Chaturanga
Principle: Surrender Scripture:
Romans 12: 1; James 4:7, 10

Pose 6 – Bjujangasana
Principle: Listening Scripture:
John 10:4, 27; James 1:5

Pose 7 – Adho Mukha Svanasana
Principle: Strength Scripture: Psalm
73:26; Joshua 1:9; Isaiah 41:10b

Pose 8 – Ardha Uttanasana
Principle: Preparation
Scripture: I Corinthians 16:13

Pose 11 – Anjali mudra
Principle: Prayer
Scripture: Job 22:27a; Philippians 4:6

Pose 12 – Padmasana
Principle: rest, stillness
Scripture: Psalm 46:10

Pose 13 – Tadasana
Principle: Strength and readiness
Scripture: Ephesians 6:10

Notes of Gratitude

To God:
I am ever grateful for Sovereign's guidance, in all of life and for giving me the vision for this book.

To CJ:
How blessed I am to have a partner as strong, supportive and stable as you! Your charming good looks are a bonus. Thank you for trying to understand all the ideas in my head.

To my parents David & Edwina Williams:
Thank you both also for modeling what it means to develop a personal relationship with God.

To my BSFs, my biggest supporters:
Thank you for seeing me and cheering me on.

To my brother Justin:
My loving critic and coach, thank you for every push.

To my artistry team – Laura Boffa, Gloria Martin, and Balsam Zubaidi:
Laura, you are a word wizard. Thank you for your small adjustments that made big impact.
Gloria, your artwork speaks volumes. Thank you for giving life to this book.
Balsam, you are a magnificent art seamstress. You have pulled this project together so beautifully.

To my yoga teachers – Hanif Hakima of Rising Hearts Yoga, Deb Bracken of Some Like it Hot Yoga, Lex Gillian of the Yoga Institute, Inga Seals of Inga the Yoga Goddess and the HealHaus family in Brooklyn:
Thank you for helping me build and maintain a healthy yoga practice.

To my Spelman Sisters (Johnetta Cole voice):
I am ever inspired and amazed by your brilliance.

To my extraordinary family:
Your love and your humor are fuel for me. We are truly blessed.

CPSIA information can be obtained
at www.ICGtesting.com
Printed in the USA
BVRC102136240922
647841BV00025B/300

9 780578 334806